FASHION IN THE 60's

FASHION IN THE 60's

Barbara Bernard

ACADEMY EDITIONS · LONDON
ST. MARTIN'S PRESS · NEW YORK

ACKNOWLEDGEMENTS

I would like to thank the following individuals, companies and institutions for
supplying material and for permission to reproduce photographs and drawings:
Paul Babbs; David Bailey; John Bates; Richard Branson; The British Tourist
Authority; Elliott & Sons Ltd.; George Harrap and Co. Ltd.; International Wool
Secretariat; The London College of Fashion; Mike McGrath; Madame Tussauds
Ltd.; Mary Quant Ltd.; Vidal Sassoon Ltd.; John Stephen Ltd.; Thames Television
Ltd.; Twiggy; Sally Tuffin; The Way In, Harrods Ltd.

My thanks are also due to Barbara Hulanicki for permission to reproduce from
Biba catalogues and to Mrs. Jenny Peel for the loan of the catalogues, and to
Woburn Studios Ltd. for permission to select and reproduce examples from ten
years of fashion photography.

Front cover
Courtesy T. Elliott & Sons Ltd.
Frontispiece
Jean Shrimpton — the top model of the early Sixties — in 1964 (Photograph by
David Bailey)
Opposite
Sketch of three early Quant designs: 'Pinafore pleats' (1958), 'Peachy' (1960)
and 'Rex Harrison' (1960).

First published in Great Britain in 1978 by
Academy Editions 7 Holland Street London W8

SBN 85670 369 9

First published in the USA in 1978 by
St. Martin's Press Inc
175 Fifth Avenue New York NY 10010
ISBN: 0-312-28460-8
Library of Congress Catalog Card Number 78-60788

Printed and bound in Great Britain by
Hazell, Watson & Viney Ltd Aylesbury

In 1961 the Beatles were discovered in a Liverpool cellar by Brian Epstein, who signed them up in a reckless and optimistic bid for new talent. In the same year the first discotheque opened in London, the twist became a new fad, *Private Eye* launched its own brand of irreverently satirical journalism, Peter Blake was recognised as the pioneer of pop art in Britain, and Mary Quant went wholesale, designing the first range of co-ordinates in the country. These were some of the events which marked the beginning of a decade which was to be known as the Swinging Sixties, and the end of the drab and dutiful Fifties. In every area, and above all in fashion, there was an exciting sense of change, characterised by a youthful frivolity and audacity. It is a decade which has been described as a renaissance and a revolution.

But the roots of change lay in the Fifties. The teddy boys and beatniks of the Beat Generation had sown the seeds of discontent and established a subversive energy which was to be inherited by the rockers and the fashion conscious mods. Chelsea was at the time a rundown area, inhabited by artists and young people with a taste for Bohemian life. In 1955 Mary Quant opened Bazaar, the first boutique, on the King's Road. It was financed jointly by her boyfriend (later to become her husband) Alexander Plunkett-Green and Archie McNair who had just opened Britain's first coffee bar, also on the King's Road. Between them they possessed a great love for the Chelsea set, of which they were an integral part, but knew nothing about selling clothes.

From an early Sixties knee revealing suit to mid-Sixties thigh flashing minis, and a pair of satin trousers (Woburn Studios).

On the King's Road, from *Young London* by Frank Habicht, Harrap & Co. Ltd., London.

John Bates's Dress of the Year 1965, in linen, printed in terra cotta and navy blue with a blue nylon mesh midriff. Courtesy Museum of Costume, Bath.

Opposite
Cut-away dress by Quant (John Adriaan).

After studying illustration at Goldsmiths' College, Mary Quant had taken a job with a couture milliner, where she would spend three days stitching a hat for one woman. It struck her that fashion should not exist for the privileged few but for everyone, and especially for the young. "I had always wanted young people to have a fashion of their own, absolutely Twentieth Century fashion," she wrote in her autobiography.

In an attempt to extend the meaning of fashion beyond the classical couture designs of the affluent, Mary Quant went out in search of clothes for Bazaar. In the first week the shop took five times more than she had expected, proving to her that "there was a real need for fashion accessories for young people chosen by people of their own age. The young were tired of wearing essentially the same as their mothers." Nevertheless, as a buyer she was dissatisfied with the range of clothes available to her and, inspired by the reaction to a pair of "mad house pyjamas" that she had designed for the opening (they were snatched up by *Harper's Bazaar* for an editorial and then taken by an American manufacturer to copy) she decided that the shop would have to be stocked with clothes designed and made by herself. She bought a sewing machine which she set up in her bedsitter, and soon expanded, moving to a larger bedsitter where she employed a few machinists. Her designs were a huge success. Few of the garments stayed on the rails for more than a day. Her best sellers included small white plastic collars to brighten a black sweater or dress, of which she sold thousands at 2/6d each, and black stretch stockings. She experimented with balloon style dresses and knickerbockers, violated traditional rules of good taste by mixing large spots and

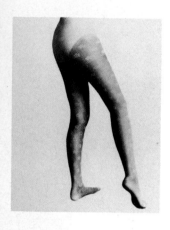

Linen mini with decorative lacing,
by John Bates.

Patterned stockings and tights,
by Quant.

Poster for Quant's Ginger Group.

Window shopping in Knightsbridge, from *Young London* by Frank Habicht, Harrap & Co. Ltd., London.

Shaded pink chiffon blouse worn as a dress *(left)* and black chiffon Thirties dress with silver and red beading *(right),* both worn by Marsha Hunt. Courtesy Richard Branson, *Student Magazine,* (Terence Donovan).

checks and, heralding the designs of the Sixties, she dropped the waistline which had clung to woman for twenty-five years as an emphasis of her femininity, subsequently eliminating it altogether in the pinafore and sack dress. Bazaar became a focal point for the Chelsea set. The Chelsea girl was clothed by Quant. "It had begun to dawn on us that by luck . . . by chance . . . perhaps even by mistake . . . we were on to a huge thing," she said. "We were in at the beginning of a tremendous renaissance in fashion."

By 1961 a second Bazaar had opened, this time in Knightsbridge. The King's Road was alive with boutiques and coffee bars, catering for the needs of a young generation who for the first time since the war had money to spend on enjoyment, and probably for the first time ever had the freedom to spend it. The Sixties promised to be affluent — there was no need to save. Moreover, a growing number of girls were working and seemed eager to spend their wage packets on clothes in which they could appeal to their bosses, and yet which felt comfortable and unrestricting. Perhaps the most fashion conscious of Sixties' youth were the mods. Fashion was central to their identity, in direct opposition to their rivals the rockers whose interest in clothes was deliberately confined to greasy leathers. "It was the mods," says Quant, "who gave the dress trade the impetus to break through the fast moving, breathtaking, uprooting revolution." There was always a need to keep pace with them. Whereas in the beginning Quant had tried to express the spirit of the tight black skirted, black stockinged, high booted, long haired Chelsea girl, in the early Sixties she was faced with the mods as a market. It was a market which, existing as it did in a larger framework, was forever growing in size and influence. Quant's fashion spread. Already there were traffic jams on the King's Road, crowds outside Bazaar where new, gawky mannequins with angular faces and long limbs stood aggressively to proclaim the coming of the Sixties look. In 1961 Quant went wholesale. It was the only way to keep prices down to a level where they were accessible to a mass market.

By 1963 Chelsea had crossed the Atlantic with Quant exporting to the USA. Contact with American fashion helped to reinforce her view that the designer should create a total look in which accessories, 'mix-and-match' separates, coats, boots, stockings — all the most and least obvious items of clothing — harmonized with each other and with the wearer to create a single impression. She called it 'the Look,' and in 1963 Vidal Sassoon arrived on the scene to complete 'the Look' with a short, angular hairstyle, 'the Bob.' In the same year Quant went into mass production to meet the demands of a US market, formed the Ginger Group, and was presented with the Sunday Times International Award for 'Jolting England Out of its Conventional Attitude Towards Clothes.'

At the same time Carnaby Street was becoming a new centre for the 'swinging' generation. Sally Tuffin and Marion Foale had left the Royal College of Art in 1961 and taken three floors of a narrow house and a shop front in Carnaby Street, a dusty Soho back street lined with empty warehouses. In the spirit of the age they shunned Paris fashion — "We suddenly didn't want to be chic; we just wanted to be ridiculous." They turned instead to 'fun' clothes. In 1962 they discovered lace and were discovered by Woolands, who put in a large order for one of their lace dress designs. Things snowballed and by 1963 they found themselves fulfilling their ambition of running a successful business without the help of a man.

Tuffin and Foale were not alone in Carnaby Street. John Stephen had come to London in the late Fifties after working in a Glasgow menswear department. He took a job at Moss Bros., and was soon able to open his own, and the first, menswear boutique in Carnaby Street. John Stephen was an important catalyst in the changing look of men's fashion. Although he confined himself at first to the traditional scheme of shirt, jacket and tie, he introduced colour and a certain flamboyancy to the style. He encouraged men to be more clothes conscious and adventurous. Fighting a basic inhibition in many men who felt that an interest in colour and cut suggested homosexuality, Stephen used as models strong masculine figures such as boxer Billy Walker. At the same time he persuaded some of the young, popular

Opposite: White lace suit by Tuffin and Foale (Peter Tebbit)

George Hammond of the Moody Blues in John Stephens crushed velvet flared trousers and suede waistcoat (Mike McGrath)

White satin Russian look shirt by John Stephen. The BBC switchboard was jammed with enquiries after Mick Avory of The Kinks, pictured here, wore it on *Top of the Pops.* (Mike McGrath)

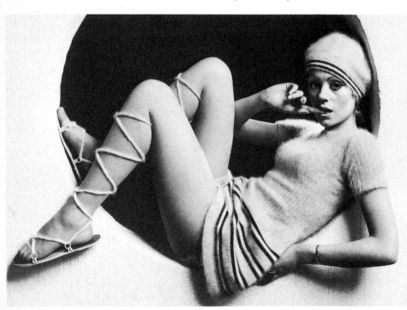

Knitted mini and hat (Woburn Studios)

John Stephens outfits for men and women (Mike McGrath)

An early Quant design

fashion publications to feature his clothes. His struggle was worthwhile. By 1966 Carnaby Street was lined with men's boutiques, nine of them owned by John Stephen. It was known as Peacock Alley.

Perhaps the most significant event in 1963 outside the field of fashion was the Profumo Affair. Journalist Peter Evans had gone so far as to say that the Swinging Sixties began at the precise moment on 22nd March, 1963, when Profumo lied to the House of Commons about his associations with Christine Keeler. In the same month the Beatles were first noticed in the

Quant design for Courtelle

charts with *Please Please Me.* By June the Beatles had reached the top of the charts twice, and Profumo had resigned. It was the old order against the new. The bastions of British society seemed to be falling from grace. Honesty and accepted morals became meaningless, *Private Eye* had a field day and Christine Keeler, an independent, confident girl became something of a heroine.

There were other heroes and heroines to replace the old — the Beatles, of course, with their 'stone age hair styles' and Chelsea boots; the Rolling Stones whose blatant aggression towards anything old and established appea-

'Fizz,' an early Quant design.

Quant Ginger Group matching coat and dress, with knitted in sleeves and collar and black patent belt. This 1964 design came in black and white, jade and orange, and turquoise and olive. Courtesy International Wool Secretariat. (IWS Photos)

Pages 24 and 25
Two 1966 Quant designs using strong 'op art' contrasts. Influenced by sports and work clothes, Quant was the first to top her skirts with braces, and to use track suits features in her designs for trousers.

Two Quant designs for Courtelle.

led to young girls and shocked their mothers; models, photographers, writers and the new fashion designers. The new heroes were young, ambitious, revolutionary in idea, and in some way classless. They came from the East End, Liverpool, Glasgow, Chelsea, and their duty was only to youth. Above all they were essentially anti-Establishment (they invented the word Establishment). It was the beginning of the permissive age. "The voices, rules and culture of this generation are as different from those of the past as tea and wine," wrote Mary Quant, "and the clothes they choose evoke their lives . . . daring, gay, never dull."

The biggest dare of all was the mini skirt. Ernestine Carter declared 1963 the Year of the Leg. The hemline rose above the knee to become the focal point of the decade. With the rising hemlines came an emphasis on the leg. Stockings were suddenly important. They took on bold textures and bright colours, for as skirts rose, legs became obviously more and more obvious. There followed 'mad patterns' and applique (instigated by John Bates who scattered rose petals over a model's stockings to match her dress). When the hemline reached its highest point tights had to be invented. High boots looked good with the new, clean lines and in the Autumn of 1963

Quant designs for Courtelle. These designs for woolly dresses and tights, as well as those on the preceeding pages, were sold as patterns to be knitted by the industrious Sixties girl — or her mother.

Two John Bates
designs for
Diana Rigg on
the *Avenger*
series. Stockings
for the series
were designed
by Echo Hosiery.
Courtesy Thames
Television.

Felicity Green in *The Daily Mirror* proclaimed: "Boots with Everything!"
In 1964, John Bates, working for Jean Varon, designed a pair of trousers
with key holes at the knees. When the leg wasn't being revealed by the mini
skirt, it was to be concealed beneath trousers — hipsters, bell bottoms, sailor
trousers — they became in the Sixties an accepted fashion garment for women.

It was Bates who, in 1965, designed a dress that won the title 'The
Smallest Dress in the World.' With skirts getting shorter, armholes receding
into the shoulder, and no frills or pleats or ruffles to speak of, there didn't
seem to be much substance left to a dress. The design for which Bates won
the Dress of the Year award in 1965 had the added subtraction of a bare
midriff filled in with netting, the first hint at the see through dresses that
were to come.

In the same year John Bates was given the job of designing Diana
Rigg's costumes for ATV's Avenger series. It was to be a change of image for
the programme. They wanted something right up to date, something slick
and slightly aggressive to replace the leather cat suits and flowing gowns of
the old series, which seemed to be loosing impact. Bates designed a range of
clothes that made front page headlines in nearly every English daily, boosted
viewership for the series, and in so doing introduced 'the Look' into thousands of homes. The clothes had simple, hard lines, confidently belted
trousers and white boots, straight close fitting dresses with hemlines well

Sally Tuffin (right), and Marion Foale (left).

Opposite
Double 'D' — a 1966 Tuffin and Foale design in linen.

above the knee, white stockings, bold black and white designs. The production team complained that the skirts were too short and surreptitiously lowered the hemlines. Bates defiantly stopped leaving a hem. The camera men claimed that the TV screens could not, technically, cope with the black and white designs, but they were proved wrong. Op art had found its way into fashion and was there to stay until pop art took over. Dresses, handbags, shoes, boots, sunglasses — whole outfits emerged looking like Mondrian paintings. Everything became very graphic. It was in keeping with other areas of design, in particular with the new architecture that was rising up in

increasing heights of concrete, glass and steel. Bates was perhaps influenced by these designs; others were inspired by the work of fellow students in disciplines such as painting or sculpture at art school, especially at the Royal College of Art, springboard for many young Sixties designers and a centre of artistic and industrial innovation.

One such designer was Ossie Clarke, who claims to have been influenced also by his study of building at technical college. After completing a fashion course under Janey Ironside at the Royal College of Art, Clarke designed a collection for Alice Pollock's Quorum, his wife, Celia Birtwell, designing the

'Cilla' — gymslip mini with schoolgirl black tights, by John Bates.

prints. He later became a partner in Quorum. Intent on having the freedom to experiment with fresh ideas he designed only for the new, slim youth. He competed with the others for the shortest hemline and the most cut away armhole. He bared a few backs, created the see through dress, and was hailed as the King of the King's Road.

Fashion drawings by John Bates.

1965 was the year of Youthquake. A large American firm, Puritan Fashions, recognizing the vast talent in London, decided to export a slice of the swinging city to the States. Mary Quant, Tuffin and Foale, a handful of models and crates of clothes were transported transatlantic for what seemed like one long, crazy and contagious fashion show. Pursuing a trend she had

Three designs for Twiggy-shaped girls, by John Bates.

started in England, Quant presented her designs in a way totally removed from the traditional fashion show. There was to be no demure toe-stepping down the cat walk. Each show started with a bang and continued with music, action, everything fast and jazzy. The shows were planned and rehearsed to echo perfectly the spirit of the clothes. Quant's fashion shows, like

Sixties chick — fashion drawing by John Bates.

her window displays, were events or 'happenings' which anticipated the happenings of the late Sixties. The Americans loved it; to them it was a new concept in fashion. Tuffin and Foale introduced them to the bicycle dress, the trouser suit, op art prints, curtain lace suits, and their famous 'gruyere' designs with holes in the sleeves. Quant had just brought out a rainwear

Sassoon hairstyle,1966, with make-up to match (Barry Lategan).

range in which p.v.c. was for the first time used as a fashion fabric. The look was described in glowing terms by Puritan's PR team: "Fluid skimmers that wing over the figure sans a defined waistline, short short hemlines, architectural hairdos a la Vidal Sassoon, teeny tiny little sling-back shoes. It all adds up to a little boy look, an almost gangling adolescent look." London had become the focal point for the world of fashion.

'Asymetric Isadora' — 1968 hairstyle by Sassoon (Hans Feurer).

Satin hipsters and shirt by Quant — with a Sassoon hairstyle and pencilled lashes to complete 'the Look.'

Licked!

That's the new lip look.
Just licked. Moist. Lush. Pearly.
Only the new Mary
Quant Brush Lipsticks are made
to give you lips like that.
Soft enough. Glossy enough.
In the eight great
shades of the moment. The only
ones you need right now.
Any one of them could lick
any man in the room.

MARY QUANT

7s 9d

9s 9d

'Licked' — pearly lip look by Quant.

Jean Shrimpton, 1962 (David Bailey)

Opposite
Jean Shrimpton, 1963 (David Bailey)

At the turn of the year London was contemplating the hemline. Griggs predicting fashion in *The Daily Mail,* looked to a John Bates design for clues. "The hem of this dress," she wrote, "is somewhere around the hip-bone . . . but there are matching tights in the same op art fabric to make it all less scandalous." For the following year she forecast p.v.c. boots, shorter skirts colours of the rainbow and op art. She was right. The mini became the controversial subject of the year, a popular topic of conversation and frequent subject for newspaper coverage. When Cheryl Thornton appeared on the David Jacobs Show it was decided that her mini was too short for family viewing before nine p.m. When Cathy McGowan, pop priestess, fashion idol and compere of the TV pop show Ready Steady Go, threatened to appear in a long coat, the British Society for the Preservation of the Mini Skirt was formed to demonstrate outside the television studios. In September of 1966 the society rallied outside Christian Dior where the new collection, featuring long coats and dresses, was about to be introduced. The four demonstrators

The cut Sassoon took to New York for the opening of his Madison Avenue salon in 196
– styled by Roger Thompson of Sassoon (Barry Lategan).

Opposite
An everyday Sixties face, with unstyled hair and pencilled lashes (Woburn Studios)

Interior of Biba, High Street Kensington, where not only clothes, but cane chairs, luxurious cushions, lampshades and artificial flowers were sold — the total look for the late Sixties. Courtesy British Tourist Authority.

carried banners proclaiming 'Mini Skirts Forever' and 'Support the Mini.' Their president Bill Scharf, claiming a membership of four hundred and fifty mini skirt enthusiasts, said that the society existed 'for the good of mankind.'

But the Society for the Preservation of the Mini Skirt had little to fear for the time being. 'The Look' was firmly established. *Time Magazine* came to London in 1966 to document it and described a city "pulsating with half a dozen separate veins of excitement," where dresses were three to six inches above the knee. They went to Bazaar, to Granny Takes a Trip where pop art was gaining ground, and to Guys and Dolls coffee bar on the King's Road where they found "a pretty blonde teen-ager, her yellow and black p.v.c. . . . and mini skirt hiked over patterned stockings."

They also went to Biba. Biba was started as a mail order business in 1964 by fashion designer Barbara Hulanicki and her ad man husband Stephen Fitzsimon, in an attempt to cater for a mass teenage market. They felt that, despite the efforts of Mary Quant and other young designers, the price of fashion was still too high for many. Clothes were relatively cheap, but at the rate styles were changing it was not easy for some, especially the newly fashion conscious schoolgirls, to keep up. Biba promoted the 'knock-down, throw-away-and-buy-another' philosophy. The cheaper the clothes the more temporary they could be. When Felicity Green in *The Mirror* featured one of Biba's gingham dresses at just under three pounds, the orders flooded in. As a result of this success Barbara Hulanicki opened Biba as a small boutique in

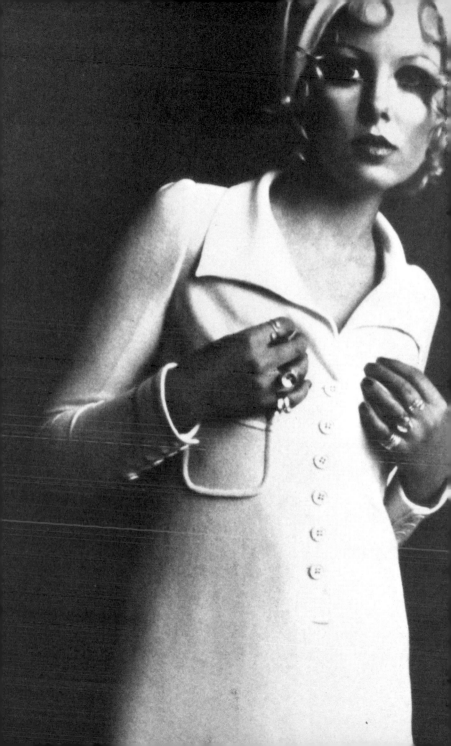

'Fun' furs — and chilly knees — for Sixties' winters (Woburn studios).

All colour illustrations are from Biba catalogues. (Hans Feurer and Helmut Newton)

John Stephen's furry look (Mike McGrath).

Abingdon Road. She brightened up the first order of black dresses with brai
kept the prices down, and found that the shop was constantly full. In 196
Biba opened in Kensington Church Street.

Hulanicki, like Quant, was concerned with the total look. She liked tl
new, skinny shape and designed clothes that would emphasise it. Her dress
had high armholes, narrow sleeves cut in on the shoulder and flared skir
She designed co-ordinates in subtle colour combinations with an empha:
on 'sludge' tones — prunes, plums, greys. She was a huge success. Peop
would wait for vans to arrive with new designs. Cathy McGowan wore

John Stephon outfits (Mike McGrath).

different Biba dress for each weekly TV show, Biba became a way of life. The shop itself had been designed with the greatest care. It was dark like a disco-theque with a hi-fi system playing rock music. There were dark mahogany screens everywhere, twenty potted palms, and twenty nine hat stands laden with hats, feathers and assorted clothes.

Twiggy was the epitome of 'the Look' when *The Daily Express* launched her as the Face of '66. She was only seventeen, but she had been photograp-hed by Barry Lategan, had had her hair cut by Vidal Sassoon, had saved up for Ossie Clarke and Biba dresses, and had worked as a model under a year's

A John Stephen 'Eastern' waistcoat (Mike McGrath).

Men's shoes (Mike McGrath)

Crochet tops and striped cotton skirt and trousers by John Stephen, 1965 (Mike McGrath)

John Stephen's answer, in 1968, to irate bosses and nagging headmasters — men's wigs for evening and weekend wear. John Stephen is pictured here with his own hair (top left), and three wigs (Mike McGrath).

Kaftan suits with mandarin collars and 'Eastern' patterns, by John Stephen (Mike McGrath).

contract to *Woman's Mirror,* who were interested in using young, new, thin faces. Twiggy was the perfect model for the time. She weighed six and a half stone and took size six in dresses. She was flat chested and stick legged, she was guaranteed to look good in a mini. She had a small, thin face capped with a boyish haircut and large dark eyes underlined with pencilled lashes. She was a natural model of the perfect Sixties shape described by John Bates in 1965 — "Narrow body, perfect square shoulders, long legs, small bust." Twiggy was booked by *Elle* magazine and *Vogue,* and within a few months was Britain's most sought after model. Film and record companies wanted her to act and record for them, manufacturers asked her to endorse clothes and cosmetic products. Her line "It's not what you'd call a figure, is it?" became a standard joke, and suddenly everyone was slimming.

By the end of 1966 Twiggy had been voted Woman of the Year and Mary Quant had received the OBE for her contribution to the fashion industry. Twiggy was unable to attend the presentation due to a nervous teenage rash; Mary Quant turned up at the Palace in a mini and cut away gloves. The old order was coming to accept the rebel youth culture. But unavoidably this culture was being absorbed by the Establishment and capitalised upon by large manufacturers throughout the country.

In 1967 Twiggy modelled extensively in France, Japan and the States. Twiggy doubles were springing up as far away as Australia, and her image had been plastered over walls, magazine pages and televison screens. A wholesale manufacturer, Taramina Textiles, contracted ex-Royal College of Art students Paul Babs and Pamela Proctor to design a 'Twiggy' range of clothes which were to be distributed to large stores throughout Britain. Paper

Plastic dress designed by John Bates in 1965, modelled by Twiggy.

Opposite
Twiggy modelling in Japan. Courtesy Paul Babbs and Twiggy.

Pages 66 and 67
Twiggy in two of Paul Babbs's 'Twiggy Range' designs. Courtesy Taramina Textiles (Barry Lategan)

Above
Twiggy, modelling
in Japan. Courtesy
Paul Babbs and
Twiggy.

Left
Twiggy in wax
at Madame
Tussauds.
Courtesy
Madame Tussauds
Ltd., London.

Mary Quant (in sunglasses), Alexander Plunket-Greene, and friends of Bazaar in 1963, showing one of Quant's most influential designs, 'Snob,' from the first Ginger Group collection (second dress from the right).

dresses had come and gone; p.v.c., false eyelashes and high boots were nothing new, and Quorum had dropped the hemline. There was a need for something different. By the summer of 1967 London was ablaze with colour — pink and orange, pink and purple, yellow and red — all the most shocking combinations. Not all of this colour belonged to Quant or Biba or the mass manufacturers. Much of it took the form of ex-army regimental uniform bought second hand from the new Portobello Road or Chelsea antique markets. Men were wearing them about town with white jeans and corduroys and, as Christopher Ward reported in *The Mirror,* "with all that gold and scarlet braid they do look rather good." Men were growing their hair and breaking away from the shirt and jacket, and girls were joining them at the secondhand stalls in search of old velvet, feathers, beaded and sequined blouses to wear as dresses, and as many beads and bangles as possible. Compared with these "baubles, bangles, beads and bells," commented Felicity Green, "the Quant-type mini skirts pale into establishment respectability."

It was the beginning of the hippie culture and the hippie look, a revolution within a revolution. It was not a designer's fashion — most of the clothes were second-hand, besides which a large part of the attraction lay in the fact that no-one's dress was identical with anyone elses. Some designers tried briefly to approximate the hippie look. Others branched off into some-

69

'Lips' — dress design by Ossie Clarke for Quorum, in white with black spots and pink neck and sleeve bands. Courtesy Quorum.

Shoulder bag by Quant in black and white p.v.c.

Mini and knee-high suede boots (Woburn Studios)

Light cotton 'baby-doll' mini (Woburn Studios).

'Bring Back the Lash' — Quant cosmetic advertisement for false eyelashes.

Tuffin and Foale dress designs (Sidney Pizan)

thing new; Tommy Roberts, for instance, whose shop Mr. Freedom in Kensington Church Street specialised in T-shirts zig-zagged in bright colours and flashes of silver. Mr. Fish opened his menswear shop in the King's Road and designed Beau Brummell shirts with ruffles and large collars for the select few. He invented the kipper tie, the Russian influenced shirt with fastenings on one side, and roll topped silk shirts. He, like John Stephen, had to fight at first against fears of effeminacy — "how many people here," he challenged "are man enough to wear a pink shirt?" — yet soon his styles were being copied for mass production and sold to the man about town.

The end of the Sixties saw a gradual diversification and breakdown of 'the Look.' The people who had created and become involved in that initial

Top left
Dress by Tuffin and Foale.

Top right
Skin hugging mini in striped jersey (Woburn Studios).

Below
Dresses in lace and wool (Woburn Studios).

Opposite
'Op art' dresses with cut-away armholes, by Chloe. Courtesy International Wool Secretariat (IWS Photos).

Page 80
Embroidered shawl worn by Marsha Hunt. Courtesy Richard Branson (Terence Donovan)

Page 81
Wrap-over dress with fringing, by Tuffin and Foale (James Wedge).

Three-piece linen suit by Tuffin and Foale, 1966.

revolutionary phase — the mods, the Chelsea girls, the High Street girls — were going their separate ways. They were growing up. At the end of 1967 there was some doubt as to the future of the mini. Fashion columns suggested the 'mini-maxi, in times of confusion,' a strange skirt design onto which a separate piece could be added to alter the length. In 1968 the maxi gained a considerable following. It was thought particularly sensible in the wintertime. The old clothes trend continued, extending in the Winter to old fur coats and

Butterfly dress and bonnet by Rimka, 1966.

granny shawls. The face was changing. Mary Quant had brought out a range of cosmetics which broke away from the pale faced, candy lipped, dark eyed mask, presenting instead a more natural look. Similarly plastic and p.v.c. came to be frowned upon as artificial. There was a growing disillusionment amongst the young with the modernities that the affluent Sixties had brought. a feeling central to the culture of the hippies who went to India and Afghanistan bringing back samples of ornate Eastern clothes which not only triggered

'Clothes you can both get into' — 1969 unisex clothes poster.
Courtesy Way in, Harrods Ltd.

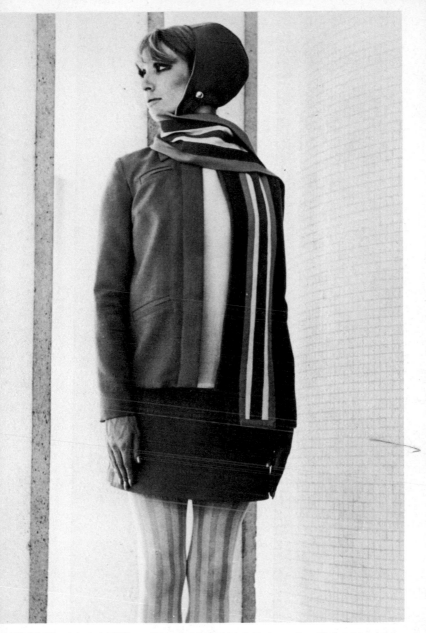

'Mid Thigh Theatricals,' 1966 — mix-and-match skirt, jacket, scarf and helmet by John Bates, in combinations of red, orange, bright pink, mustard, white and lime. Courtesy International Wool Secretariat (IWS Photos).

Corduroy
Trench Coat
and skirt

T Shirt dress
and college scarf

Polo dress
and jerkin

Hacking jacket set

Cotton jersey
cardigan set

Negligee and nightie

Pirate set

Biba blue catalogue, back cover. Courtesy Barbara Hulanicki.

off yet another fashion trend, but were to have a strong influence on British designers. As a natural progression from changes in both women's and men' roles, unisex, the jeans and T-shirt look, became a growing cult. What with men wearing their hair long and women's figures shaped by the Twiggy look it was reputed to be hard to distinguish a boy from a girl. Quant and Quorun and John Bates, ten years older, were tending towards more sophisticated designs (although Quant did invent hot pants to see the Sixties out). And at the end of 1969 Biba, now opened on a grand scale in Kensington High Street, was concentrating on the Thirties look with lots of satin, ostrich feathers and long dresses.

The mini became a midi and the midi became a maxi. By the Seventies the controversy of the hemline had become obscured by more serious matters efore long, 'the Look' seemed dated. But today's fashion could not have eveloped without the revolution of the Sixties; and our boutiques, bistros, offee bars and discotheques are all a heritage of that decade. We have inerited the concept of the total look, with accessories — right down to sunlasses, watches, legwear, belts and buckles and underwear — matching the entiment of the clothes to create a particular effect. Even interiors became, n the Sixties, a part of the fashion look, with Quant and Biba designing and narketing paints, wallpapers, furnishing fabrics, waste paper bins and posters. Record covers, book jackets, magazine graphics and illustration, influenced y important young designers such as Peter Blake and Alan Aldridge, shook ff the dust of decades and 'went pop.' Fashion and design became a matter f concept more than merely good taste. Whereas the woman of the Fifties vas primarily concerned with matching a blue handbag to blue shoes and lue gloves, with daywear and eveningwear, Summer Seasons and Winter easons, fashion in the Sixties cut across such divisions concentrating instead n the 'school-girl look,' 'op art look,' 'hippie look,' 'the Twenties look.' And behind every concept lay the idea of fun.

Mary Quant, John Bates, Ossie Clarke, and many other Sixties designers ontinue to influence the fashion of today. The young photographers Bailey, ategan, Donovan, who did so much to consolidate the look of the decade, re still top photographers in the Seventies. Twiggy has become a TV persoality and singer, and the four Beatles, nearing middle age, are still singing.

Biba motif. Courtesy Barbara Hulanicki.